TIME FOR KIDS READERS

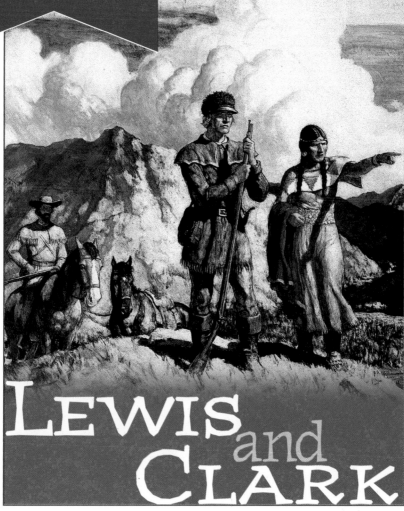

LEWIS and CLARK

by Susan Ring

Harcourt
SCHOOL PUBLISHERS

Orlando   Austin   New York   San Diego   Toronto   London

Visit *The Learning Site!*
www.harcourtschool.com

In 1801 Thomas Jefferson was President of the United States. At the time, the United States looked very different than it does today. The land west of the Mississippi River had not been explored by U.S. citizens.

As President, Jefferson hoped to expand the borders of the United States as far west as the Pacific Ocean.

Thomas Jefferson

In 1803 the United States bought the Louisiana Territory, which covered more than 800,000 square miles, from the French. The sale totaled about $15 million and became known as the Louisiana Purchase. Jefferson asked Congress for money to pay for an expedition to explore the new territory.

This is how the United States looked in 1803. Which present-day states are not on this map?

The Expedition Sets Out

It was going to be a long and dangerous trip, and Jefferson needed people he could count on to do the job. He chose Meriwether Lewis and William Clark to lead a group of about 30 soldiers. Both men had been in the army. Lewis had worked for Jefferson at one time, and Clark was Lewis's good friend.

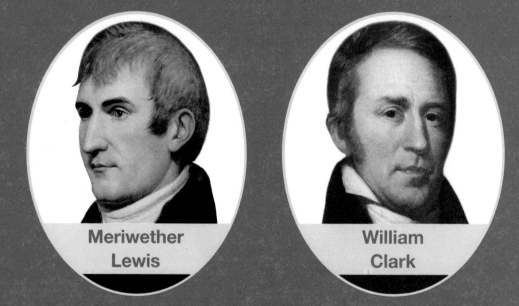

Meriwether Lewis

William Clark

The journey began as the group, called the Corps of Discovery, left its camp near St. Louis on May 14, 1804. The goal of the journey was to explore the land west of the Mississippi River. Jefferson also wanted to know if it was possible to travel to the Pacific Ocean by following the Missouri and Columbia rivers.

Mississippi River

Lewis and Clark were both strong leaders, but their leadership styles were different. Lewis liked to walk on the riverbank ahead of everyone. Clark guided the boat along the river.

Both Lewis and Clark kept diaries to record their experiences. They saw prairie dogs, pronghorn antelope, coyotes, and grizzly bears for the first time. Upon seeing a coyote for the first time, Clark called it a prairie wolf.

This compass was used by Lewis and Clark on their trip. It helped them find their way.

In their diaries, they wrote about the beautiful land. They also wrote about the heat and the mosquitoes. They drew pictures and kept track of the weather and geography.

By October the explorers reached what is now North Dakota. Travel turned out to be more difficult than they expected. They stopped for the winter and built a camp near the Mandan and Hidatsa American Indians. During this time, the explorers learned more about the land ahead.

A Mandan village

From 1804 to 1806, William Clark wrote and drew in this diary.

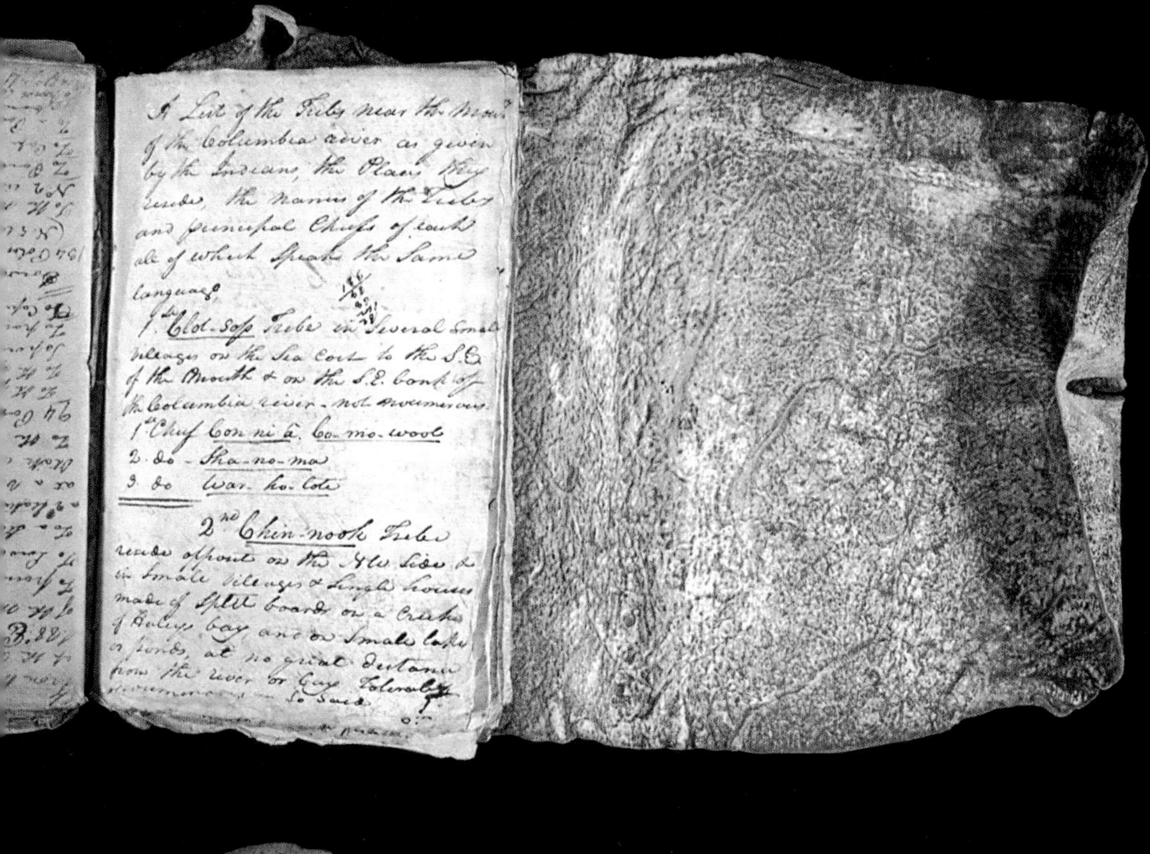

The Expedition Continues West

In the Mandan village, they met a French fur trader named Toussaint Charbonneau (TOO•sant SHAR•bon•oh) and his wife, a Shoshone (shoh•SHOH•nee) woman named Sacagawea (sa•kuh•juh•WEE•uh). These two people helped guide Lewis and Clark on their travels through the wilderness ahead.

In April 1805, the explorers left the Mandan and continued west. Sacagawea guided them and also picked wild fruit and plants for the travelers to eat.

Sacagawea, whose name in Shoshone means "Bird Woman," traveled with her baby son on her back.

As they crossed over miles of unexplored land, they met a group of Shoshones. To their surprise, it turned out that the Shoshone chief was Sacagawea's brother, whom she had not seen in five years. With Sacagawea's help the explorers got horses from the Shoshones to help them cross the Rocky Mountains.

A journey across the Rocky Mountains was very difficult. The travelers did not have much food, the trails were difficult, and snowstorms blinded them. Finally they made it across the mountains and came to the Clearwater River.

The Clearwater River is in what is now the state of Idaho.

Once they reached the Columbia River, Lewis and Clark knew they were on their way to the Pacific Ocean. In November 1805, they finally reached the Pacific Ocean after traveling for more than a year. Some of the travelers cried tears of joy and relief, while others got on their knees and prayed. The journey wasn't over yet, however.

The group had to turn around and return to St. Louis. They said goodbye to Sacagawea and Charbonneau when they got back to the Mandan village. They continued on and arrived in St. Louis in the fall of 1806.

Lewis and Clark saw the Pacific Ocean from the coast of Oregon, just as people standing on this hill can see it today. Which part of this view did the explorers not see?

The Oregon Trail

WASHINGTON

OREGON

IDAHO

WYOMING

NEBRASKA

KANSAS

Cascade Range

ROCKY

MOUNTAINS

GREAT

PLAINS

Columbia River

Clearwater R.

Snake River

South Pass

Platte River

Missouri River

Independence

PACIFIC OCEAN

—— Oregon Trail   —— Present-day border

In 2004 the United States Postal Service issued 3 stamps to commemorate the 200th anniversary of the Lewis and Clark expedition. This stamp shows the explorers surveying the countryside. The other two show portraits of Lewis and Clark.

In the end, Lewis and Clark did not find a waterway connecting the Missouri River to the Pacific Ocean. But with their crew and the help of Sacagawea and others, they discovered much more.

We remember and honor these brave people who opened up the West to all of us.